I0427624

DEPARTMENT OF THE INTERIOR

Office of Inspector General

ASSESSMENT
OF THE
U.S. FISH AND WILDLIFE SERVICE
OFFICE OF LAW ENFORCEMENT

PI-EV-FWS-0003-2006   February 2007

United States Department of the Interior

Office of Inspector General
Washington, D.C. 20240

FEB 1 3 2007

Memorandum

To: Dirk Kempthorne
           Secretary

From: Earl E. Devaney
           Inspector General

Subject: Assessment of the Fish and Wildlife Service, Office of Law Enforcement
           Programs (No. PI-EV-FWS-0003-2006)

This memorandum transmits our report detailing the results of our assessment of the Fish and Wildlife Service Office of Law Enforcement (FWS-OLE). This assessment is part of our continuing efforts to evaluate the management of Department of the Interior law enforcement programs following the Department's initiative to reform law enforcement.

Our assessment revealed that while FWS-OLE has made significant progress in implementing mandated law enforcement reforms, further progress is needed to improve leadership and oversight, employee accountability and property accountability. The implementation of the 12 recommendations contained in this report will assist FWS-OLE management in strengthening their program.

We intend to continue to provide you and the Congress with periodic assessment reports of the Department's law enforcement and security programs. If you have any questions about this report, please do not hesitate to contact me.

TABLE OF CONTENTS

INTRODUCTION

This report presents the result of our assessment of the U.S. Fish and Wildlife Service (FWS or Service) Office of Law Enforcement (OLE). This assessment is part of ongoing efforts by the Office of Inspector General (OIG) to examine Department of the Interior (DOI or Department) law enforcement programs.

In 2001, at the request of the Secretary, we conducted a Department-wide review of law enforcement activities. In January 2002, we issued a report providing recommendations to improve leadership, organization, control, and accountability of Department law enforcement programs. In response to our report, in July 2002, the Secretary issued a series of directives to reform DOI law enforcement based on our recommendations. Since 2002, FWS-OLE has put forth efforts to implement the mandated law enforcement reforms. In fact, in our most recent progress review, we found that FWS-OLE had completed implementation of all but one of the Secretary's directives.

We began this assessment in May 2006 to conduct a more in-depth review of FWS-OLE's management and operations. We would like to acknowledge the cooperation of Department officials, FWS management, and the many employees we interviewed throughout this assessment. We witnessed the passion and dedication that FWS-OLE employees have for their profession and the FWS mission. Many FWS-OLE employees we spoke with were optimistic about what this report could do for the future of their program.

Background

The Service has a mission "to conserve, protect and enhance fish, wildlife, and plants and their habitats for the continuing benefit of the American people." FWS-OLE contributes to this mission through the enforcement of federal laws that protect wildlife resources, often working in cooperation with international, federal, state, and tribal agencies.

FWS-OLE conducts investigations, focusing on potentially devastating threats to wildlife, including illegal trade, unlawful commercial exploitation, habitat destruction, and environmental hazards. FWS-OLE also regulates wildlife trade through inspections, ensuring compliance with applicable laws and working to detect illegal trade.

FWS-OLE is comprised of approximately 208 special agents, 111 wildlife inspectors, and 166 support staff located throughout the country. Most FWS-OLE employees work in the field and report through seven regional offices headed by a Regional Special Agent in Charge (SAC). FWS-OLE's headquarters office provides direction and oversight for field operations, including issuing policy and guidance, managing budget resources, offering training opportunities, overseeing professional integrity, and providing technical expertise and administrative support (See Appendix 1 for an FWS-OLE organization chart).

Office of Law Enforcement Regions

Objective and Methodology

The objective of our assessment was to evaluate the overall accountability of the FWS-OLE program. We reviewed many aspects of the law enforcement program, including management, policies, partnerships with other agencies, funding, internal affairs, quality control inspections, employee conduct, property, evidence, and training. Our assessment focused on law enforcement activities as they relate to the FWS special agent program. The wildlife inspector program was not included in the scope of our review.

To accomplish our objective, we visited five of the seven regional law enforcement offices and headquarters. We also visited 9 Resident Agent-in-Charge (RAC) offices and 13 field offices, along with FWS-OLE training instructors at the Federal Law Enforcement Training Center. Throughout these site visits, we reviewed hundreds of program documents and conducted more than 110 interviews with officials of the Department and FWS, as well as federal and state partners.

We contracted with the Center for Ethical Business Cultures which, together with its partner Kenexa, developed and administered an independent survey of FWS-OLE employees to provide us with an in-depth appraisal of FWS-OLE's ethical culture (See Appendices 2 and 3 for survey results). Employees were also afforded the opportunity to provide us with their comments, concerns, and suggestions through electronic mail. We conducted our assessment in accordance with the President's Council on Integrity and Efficiency, Quality Standards for Inspections.

The Service's law enforcement program has gone through several changes over the past 5 years. With the issuance of the Secretary's directives for law enforcement reform in 2002, FWS-OLE has taken steps to improve its organizational efficiency, including the implementation of direct-line authority and the establishment of an internal affairs unit. FWS-OLE has also published a strategic plan identifying its mission, goals, and objectives, and has created performance measures to assess program effectiveness.

Stakeholders that work in cooperation with FWS-OLE are pleased with its performance. FWS regional managers we interviewed stated that despite organizational changes, FWS-OLE continues to work collaboratively with regional offices to fulfill the FWS mission. In addition, all of the federal and state law enforcement partners we spoke with described having a good working relationship with FWS-OLE.

With the implementation of direct-line authority, FWS-OLE unified its command structure, centralizing most of its administrative functions at the headquarters level. Despite this change in structure, we found that regions continue to operate as "seven kingdoms" with relative autonomy from headquarters' oversight. Many of the people we spoke with described an environment that lacks decisive leadership from senior management, with one interviewee stating that "the ship is rudderless at the top."

Our review discovered weaknesses in the core areas of leadership and oversight, contributing to a general mistrust of senior management. We found a lack of effective communication between FWS-OLE headquarters and the field, which has created a perception that there is a "wall" between management and field personnel. A lack of formal quality control inspections has added to these communication issues. Such inspections are not only critical in evaluating the quality of operations, but are an important tool for information flow between headquarters and the field.

Throughout our assessment, concerns were raised about the organization's culture of ethics and integrity. We also found weaknesses in internal affairs policy, and when reviewing internal affairs cases we discovered problems with investigative independence. Decentralized management of disciplinary action has created inconsistencies, resulting in agent frustration. In addition, management has not always carried out disciplinary action in a timely manner.

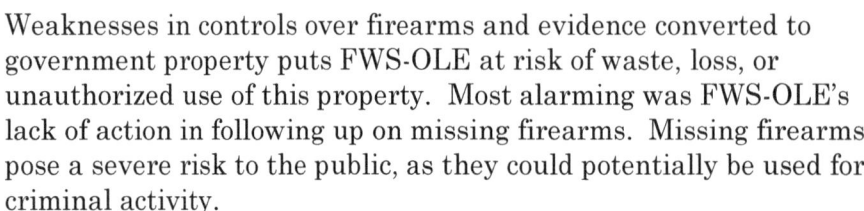

Weaknesses in controls over firearms and evidence converted to government property puts FWS-OLE at risk of waste, loss, or unauthorized use of this property. Most alarming was FWS-OLE's lack of action in following up on missing firearms. Missing firearms pose a severe risk to the public, as they could potentially be used for criminal activity.

The employee survey results supported our assessment findings. Employees gave senior leadership low marks with regard to trust and behaving in a way that is consistent with the mission. Employees were most critical about the sharing of information at FWS-OLE. That having been said, with an extraordinary response rate of 88 percent, the survey demonstrated that FWS-OLE employees are highly committed to the agency and have a strong interest in the program's future.

LEADERSHIP AND OVERSIGHT

Strong leaders are essential to inspire and motivate employees to embrace change and undertake new challenges. Conversely, ineffective leadership can stifle growth, create frustration, and prevent an agency from reaching its goals. At FWS-OLE, ineffective leadership and oversight have created what some refer to as "seven kingdoms" rather than a cohesive law enforcement organization. Although management has effectively ensured employee awareness of the FWS-OLE mission and goals, we found weaknesses in communication, quality control, and employee recognition. These weaknesses have contributed to employee frustration and ultimately a lack of trust in senior management.

Communication

Only one third of FWS-OLE survey respondents agreed that communication is open and information is shared freely within the organization.

A lack of communication between FWS-OLE senior management and field personnel has significantly impacted morale and trust, and caused many agents to question the integrity and leadership of their senior managers. While senior managers have been very successful in communicating FWS-OLE's mission, they have been less successful in keeping field personnel informed of decisions that affect their day-to-day operations. This was supported in our survey results with only a third of survey respondents agreeing that communication is open and information is shared freely within FWS-OLE.

Field personnel we interviewed explained that they have little or no contact with the FWS-OLE Chief and Deputy Chief and that a headquarters official has never visited their office. This lack of communication was also found at the regional level. Communication between field agents and their Regional SAC varies from region to region and is largely dependent on the agent's proximity to the regional office. Many field agents told us that their SAC rarely, if ever, visits their office. Most communications are directed through the agent's immediate supervisor, the RAC. While RACs frequently communicate with field agents, we found that even some RACs seldom visit the field offices under their jurisdiction.

5

When site visits are conducted, they tend to carry a negative connotation. We were told by some agents that they do not want their SAC to visit because it usually means that there is something wrong. Site visits are viewed as a reactive measure used to address a specific problem, rather than proactive by providing information and acquiring feedback from the field. One SAC even admitted that site visits are only conducted when there is an issue that needs to be dealt with. When questioned about the reason for their lack of site visits, one SAC told us that funding is better spent on other program areas.

The seven Regional SACs meet quarterly, referred to as "the Circle of Seven" by some field agents; the SACs seldom report the results of these meetings back to the field. While periodic management meetings are essential for many reasons, the necessity of FWS-OLE's quarterly meetings has become clouded. Without management feedback to the field, agents have questioned the benefits of these conferences and the resulting drain on the agency's budget.

The void in communication was also apparent when it came to the fundamental area of policy. We were told by the SAC responsible for policy that the status and availability of policy is better than it has ever been. Yet, numerous agents we spoke with and received e-mails from expressed frustration with outdated and redundant policy. Many stated that they have been waiting for years for a new policy manual and are often confused by numerous policy documents, including manual sections, Director's Memoranda, and Chief's Directives. The SAC in charge of policy stated that about half of the manual is updated and they are issuing chapters as they are completed.

The lack of communication to the field over recent disciplinary decisions and the apparent disparity in punishment between regions for similar infractions has affected morale agency-wide. Field personnel have relied on rumors and half truths in forming opinions on disciplinary actions. We understand that management is precluded from releasing some information on personnel actions; however, they have failed to address concerns voiced by field personnel that have resulted from these actions. Unresolved, these issues have festered,

allowing rumors to abound and polarizing field personnel who further question management. In fact, the employee survey revealed that less than half of FWS-OLE employees trust senior management. FWS-OLE management can, without discussing case specifics, communicate a message of what is acceptable and unacceptable

6

conduct, promoting a culture of ethics and integrity and, ultimately, building agency morale and much needed trust in senior management.

The former Chief of FWS-OLE acknowledged that more outreach is needed on a national level. In August 2006, the former Chief began sending out bi-monthly e-mails to report recent organizational developments to the field. While this is a step in the right direction, more work needs to be done to improve trust and morale throughout the program.

Recommendation

1. FWS-OLE management should develop and execute plans to improve communication throughout the organization. Plans should consider periodic site visits by all levels of management, methods to identify and address employee concerns, and centralized methods for dissemination of agency information and policy.

Quality Control

FWS-OLE has not conducted formal quality control inspections since 2001. Prior to 2001, routine inspections of FWS-OLE offices were conducted by the Training and Inspection Branch. We were told that inspections stopped occurring with the implementation of direct-line authority. FWS-OLE believed that changes in its reporting structure required that modifications be made to the inspection process.

FWS-OLE has drafted policy that modifies the inspection process and creates standards for conducting inspections. FWS-OLE is waiting for this policy to be finalized before beginning inspections; management was unable to provide us with an exact issue date for this policy. Both the former Chief and current Acting Chief attributed delays to the fact that the SAC position in charge of Training and Inspections is currently vacant. However, we were told that this position has only been vacant since early 2006. While we were told that quality control inspections will be performed beginning in 2007, management did not have any detailed plans on what inspections will be initiated and/or completed.

The importance of inspections for law enforcement agencies is clearly defined in the Commission on Accreditation for Law Enforcement Agencies, Inc. standards. These recognized law enforcement standards state a formal "inspection process is an essential mechanism for evaluating the quality of the agency's operations; ensuring that the agency's goals are being pursued; identifying the need for additional resources; and ensuring that control is maintained throughout the agency." Inspections further benefit the agency by providing senior management and supervisors with a means of regularly assessing the agency's efficiency and effectiveness.

Recommendations

2. FWS-OLE should issue policy addressing quality control inspection standards and requirements.

3. FWS-OLE should conduct formal quality control inspections annually and devise a plan for inspections to be completed at all FWS-OLE locations in the next 3 years.

Employee Advancement and Recognition

Only 37% of FWS-OLE employees agreed with the following statement:

"Where I work, people don't 'get ahead' unless their behavior clearly demonstrates FWS-OLE values."

FWS-OLE needs to improve efforts to recognize those employees that demonstrate organizational values. The employee survey found that less than half of FWS-OLE employees agree that demonstrating organizational values is important in determining promotions and performance ratings. Even more disturbing, is that only 37 percent of employees agreed with the following statement: "Where I work, people do not 'get ahead' unless their behavior clearly demonstrates FWS-OLE values."

When it comes to getting ahead, what appears to dictate promotions into FWS-OLE management positions is an unwritten requirement to have 2 years of experience at headquarters. Many employees we spoke with expressed frustration with this requirement, stating that SAC and ASAC positions are often awarded to agents with little or no supervisory experience. A former agent stated that managers "don't need to know how to do the job, with Washington Office time served they are divined to lead." A group of employees who provided us with written comments were so discouraged with FWS-OLE's hiring and promotion practices, they went so far as to suggest that the OIG should oversee the selection process for every FWS-OLE vacancy.

When asked about this unwritten requirement, the former Chief of FWS-OLE stated that those who have served at headquarters are much more competitive in the hiring process because of the experiences that they receive while in Washington, D.C. While we understand the benefit of having headquarters experience, this experience does not always create an effective leader or manager. We were told that supervisors receive 40 to 80 hours of supervisory training within the first 2 years as a supervisor, and additional supervisory training is provided at annual in-service training. However, given the volume of comments received regarding inexperienced managers, there appears to be a need for a more formal leadership and management development program.

We found that FWS-OLE does not have a centralized process for handling or funding performance awards. Instead, performance awards are funded through each region's operational budget. Each SAC has the discretion to recognize employees receiving an annual performance rating of superior (level 4) or exceptional (level 5) with a monetary award, a quality-step increase, a time-off award, or, if they choose, no award. While we understand the benefits of a SAC's discretion, there is a negative ripple effect among employees when inconsistencies in performance awards are substantial.

We found significant inconsistencies in the issuance of performance awards, both among and within regions. Specifically, in 2005, approximately 50 percent of all FWS-OLE employees who received a performance

**Range of Monetary Performance Awards
2005**

HEADQUARTERS	$1,500-$3,500 / $0-$4,054
REGION 7	N/A / $0-$2,000
REGION 6	N/A / $0-$2,000
REGION 5	N/A / $0-$1,500
REGION 4	$1,467-$1,500 / $765-$2,000
REGION 3	$2,127-$4,850 / $1,000-$2,000
REGION 2	$1,700 / $0-$2,263
REGION 1	$1,237-$1,557 / $0-$2,263

EXCEPTIONAL PERFORMANCE RATING (LEVEL 5)

SUPERIOR PERFORMANCE RATING (LEVEL 4)

rating of exceptional were located in one region with the remaining six regions and headquarters sharing the remaining 50 percent. Additionally, in three of the regions and at FWS-OLE headquarters, agents with a performance rating of superior received higher monetary awards than those employees with a performance rating of exceptional.

We also noted discrepancies between regions on the percentage of employees receiving performance awards. In 2005, the percentage of employees receiving performance awards ranged from 9 percent in one region to 62 percent in another. We noted that Region 3, whose employees received the highest percentage of performance awards, was

9

the most critical of FWS-OLE during our survey (See Appendix 3 for regional survey results). We believe this demonstrates that excessive awards do not substitute for the importance of employee trust, open communication, and effective leadership.

Current inconsistencies in FWS-OLE performance awards may be rectified by recent Departmental policy issued during our assessment. This policy provides specific requirements for the issuance of monetary awards relating to employee performance and establishes thresholds for these awards. This policy will not, however, rectify the inconsistencies in the number of awards provided by each region.

Recommendations

4. FWS-OLE should create a formal leadership and management development program that values both headquarters and field management experience.

5. FWS-OLE should monitor the issuance of performance awards to ensure consistency among regions and ensure that new Departmental standards are followed.

Our office has investigated several allegations of misconduct by FWS-OLE special agents, including a cheating scandal and egregious misuse of government property. The significance of these investigations, as well as management's lenient response to them, caused us to begin to question FWS-OLE's culture in regards to ethics and integrity.

Strengthening the professional integrity of its workforce is one of FWS-OLE's strategic objectives. FWS-OLE's internal affairs component, referred to as the Professional Responsibility Unit (PRU), is a key factor for FWS-OLE in accomplishing this objective. While investigating allegations of misconduct is important, ultimately holding agents accountable for their actions is crucial in demonstrating and protecting organizational integrity.

Professional Responsibility Unit

The PRU was established in June 2003 to investigate allegations of misconduct by FWS-OLE employees, as well as those in the law enforcement chain of command in the FWS National Wildlife Refuge System (NWRS). Since their establishment, the PRU has opened 30 cases involving FWS-OLE special agents. These 30 cases, 3 of which were investigated by the OIG, resulted from allegations made against 28 special agents. Allegations have been sustained against 17 of those 28 agents (See chart to the right for more detail).

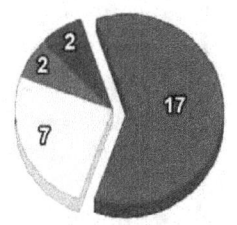

Outcome of PRU Cases Involving Special Agents
2003-2006

■ Sustained
◻ Not Sustained
■ Pending
■ Retired

In cases involving FWS-OLE special agents, the Chief or Deputy Chief of FWS-OLE, in consultation with the PRU SAC, determines whether an allegation will be investigated by the PRU or referred to the field for investigation. When reviewing PRU case files, we found that of the 30 cases involving special agents, 11 had been referred to the field for investigation. We believe, because of the severity of some of the allegations, some of these cases should have been worked by the PRU or, at a minimum, another regional office. For example, one case involving allegations of theft of government funds was referred to the RAC who was the immediate manager of the subject in the case. A case with such serious allegations should not be referred to a location where there is such a blatant conflict of interest.

While FWS-OLE does not currently have an established policy for the PRU, draft policy does establish three categories of allegations based on the severity. The draft policy requires all allegations of impropriety be reported to the PRU, but the policy is not clear on who will conduct the investigation. In fact, the draft policy defines an investigation as "a formal review of an allegation of misconduct, **usually** [emphasis added] performed by a trained investigator." The draft policy does require that managers receive authorization from the PRU before undertaking investigative action on Category 1 or 2 allegations. Authorization is not required for managers to investigate Category 3 allegations.

When asked why some cases are referred to the field for investigation, PRU officials stated it was usually due to a lack of resources. Under the practice of referring cases to the field, the SAC is not only responsible for the investigation, but is also the deciding official for any disciplinary action that may result.

The Department's Internal Affairs Interim Policy requires that internal affairs investigations shall be conducted in accordance with the President's Council on Integrity and Efficiency and Executive Council on Integrity and Efficiency, Quality Standards for Investigations. These standards require that investigative work must be free from impairments to independence. Official, professional, or personal relationships with the employee under investigation may affect the extent and/or outcome of the investigative inquiry.

We found that a lack of resources did not only affect who investigated allegations, but also sometimes affected how investigations were conducted. We discovered instances when PRU agents conducted interviews by mail rather than in person. When we asked about these practices, we were told that there was a lack of funding for travel. The PRU does not receive an annual budget for conducting investigations and must rely on headquarters to allot funds for its investigations.

Recommendations

6.   FWS-OLE should ensure all serious allegations are investigated by either the OIG or the PRU, or an appropriately trained and independent agent.

7.   FWS-OLE should ensure that the PRU is provided with an annual budget to effectively plan and provide for necessary investigative work.

Disciplinary Action

We found disciplinary action is handled on a regional basis and not centrally managed or tracked. When an investigation or an administrative inquiry is completed on a special agent, findings are provided to the agent's manager who is responsible for determining appropriate disciplinary action for substantiated allegations.

When determining the appropriate disciplinary action for an offense, each SAC works with the human resources and solicitor's offices located in the FWS regional office. We were told that these offices work to ensure that disciplinary action is consistent with other disciplinary actions carried out within that regional office; however, they do not ensure the action is consistent among agents within FWS-OLE.

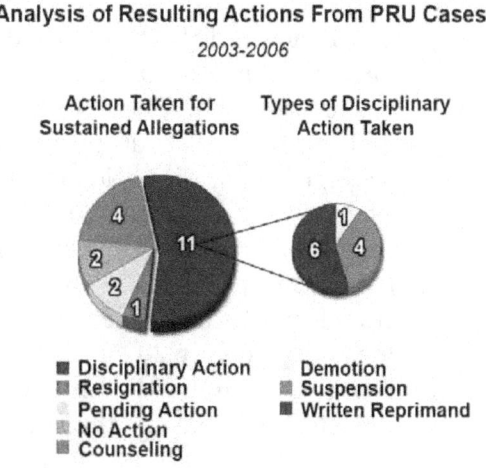

Analysis of Resulting Actions From PRU Cases
2003-2006

Action Taken for Sustained Allegations — Types of Disciplinary Action Taken

- ■ Disciplinary Action
- ■ Resignation
- Pending Action
- No Action
- ■ Counseling

- Demotion
- ■ Suspension
- ■ Written Reprimand

We found one example where an employee received the mandated 30-day suspension for misusing his/her government vehicle, while another employee located in a different region received a 14-day suspension for misusing his/her vehicle under more severe circumstances - driving the government vehicle intoxicated while in possession of his/her government firearm. We found that inconsistencies such as these have caused resentment and frustration among other FWS-OLE agents and impacted the trust placed on management.

We were told by other DOI law enforcement agencies, specifically the Bureau of Land Management and the National Park Service, that they have created centralized systems to track and compare disciplinary actions nationwide. These systems operate with senior management oversight.

In addition to inconsistencies in disciplinary action, we found instances when action to resolve employee misconduct was not carried out in a timely manner. For example, the OIG investigated allegations that an FWS-OLE special agent, while previously employed by FWS as a

13

NWRS officer, authorized a volunteer to remove a government firearm from FWS custody for the volunteer's personal use. The investigative findings were forwarded to FWS-OLE in January 2005, revealing sufficient evidence to support the allegations, including an admission by the special agent. During our review of PRU case files, we found that no action had been taken to hold the agent accountable. We brought this to the attention of a PRU official and in August 2006, 20 months after the OIG findings were forwarded to FWS-OLE, the PRU forwarded the case findings to the agent's Regional SAC for administrative action.

Our review of PRU case files also found a case where the PRU forwarded investigative findings to a Regional SAC regarding a lack of candor violation. The PRU requested that the SAC respond to the PRU by June 16, 2005, providing the nature and date of corrective action taken or the rationale why no corrective action was taken. There was no evidence of a response from the SAC in the file at the time of our review. We were referred to the former Chief of FWS-OLE to identify the cause for the SAC's delayed response. The former Chief stated that he forwarded the matter to the DOI Office of the Solicitor for review in July 2005. As of September 2006, 18 months later, the former Chief of FWS-OLE had not followed up with the Office of the Solicitor to determine the status of their review.

Recommendations

8. FWS-OLE should ensure that measures taken to hold employees accountable for their actions are carried out in a timely, fair, and consistent manner.

9. FWS-OLE should create a centralized system for handling and tracking disciplinary action of their sworn law enforcement personnel.

Strong internal controls over property are necessary to address risks associated with the waste, loss, and unauthorized use of assets. Equally important is monitoring these controls to ensure they are effective in addressing identified risks. During our assessment we found weaknesses in the accountability of firearms, as well as controls over investigative evidence that is converted to government property. These weaknesses could potentially create liability problems for FWS-OLE. Currently, FWS-OLE cannot rely on their firearms inventory systems to provide timely and accurate information. When missing weapons are discovered, FWS-OLE does not follow its own policy for investigating the whereabouts of the missing weapons.

Firearms

FWS-OLE maintains an inventory of approximately 1,330 firearms including handguns, shotguns, long rifles, and other weapons used for undercover work. Until 2003, firearms inventories were maintained regionally and there was no centralized system of accountability.

There are now two centralized inventory systems used by FWS-OLE in accounting for firearms inventory: the Personal Property Management System (PPMS) and the Law Enforcement Management Information System (LEMIS). PPMS, which is operated and maintained by the FWS Division of Contracting and Facilities Management (CFM), is the Service's official system of record for capitalized and sensitive property including firearms. FWS-OLE also maintains its own firearms inventory using LEMIS. Unlike PPMS, LEMIS is capable of tracking firearms from the time of acquisition until final disposition.

Although PPMS and LEMIS were designed to account for FWS-OLE property, FWS cannot rely on these systems to provide timely and accurate information to account for firearms issued to their agents. CFM updates PPMS only after it has received supporting acquisition, transfer, and survey documentation from FWS-OLE. Delays in receiving this supporting documentation have created a lag time in system updates, affecting the timeliness of PPMS information. We were told by one employee that PPMS is "always playing catch up."

Multiple employees with access to PPMS also threatens the reliability of information. At present, each region's Capital Property Officer can access the system and add, delete, or change information without the knowledge of the system manager. CFM has no means to identify who has entered or changed inventory information.

15

PPMS and LEMIS do not interface with each other, so information from one system cannot be accessed by the other. In addition, the firearms inventory maintained in LEMIS is unreliable because the system is not uniformly administered from region to region. PPMS and LEMIS are so unreliable that when we requested an inventory of firearms, rather than provide us a listing from either of these systems, FWS-OLE headquarters contacted each region and requested that the SAC provide them with a current inventory listing of firearms.

In centralizing its inventory process in 2003, we were told that the FWS-OLE Training and Inspection Branch found that their firearms inventory was "completely unreliable" and identified 71 firearms that were either missing, lacked supporting documentation, or were otherwise not accounted for. Since then, the FWS-OLE Training and Inspection Branch, in collaboration with CFM, has attributed 67 of the potentially 71 missing firearms identified in 2003 to paperwork errors. According to a CFM employee, the firearms inventory has improved "110 percent" in the past year and that he would give it a "B+" grade.

Despite this improvement to the firearms inventory, senior management failed to adequately follow up on the four remaining missing firearms. We discovered that two of the four missing firearms had been assigned to a former Regional SAC who left the agency in 2004. We were told there was an additional firearm attributed to this same former SAC that had originally been purchased in 1998 but had never been entered into the Service's inventory systems.

As early as February 2004, at least two of the three firearms attributed to the former SAC were reported to the FWS-OLE Chief, Deputy Chief, and the Training and Inspections Branch SAC; however, no investigation or other effort to recover the firearms was ever conducted by FWS-OLE. When asked why she did not act on this issue, one senior manager stated that property management was only one of her many job responsibilities. This was representative of management's lack of urgency to recover the firearms. Any missing firearm poses a potential risk to public safety and creates a liability for FWS-OLE.

In November 2006, after learning of the three missing firearms attributed to the former SAC, the OIG initiated an investigation. OIG investigators visited the former SAC to inquire about the firearms. We were later told by an FWS-OLE official that within an hour of the OIG investigators' visit, the former SAC contacted FWS-OLE to make arrangements to return the firearms. The fact that these weapons were out of FWS-OLE custody, with senior management's knowledge, for nearly 3 years is unacceptable.

16

In addition to being unable to account for firearms contained in FWS-OLE inventory listings, we discovered instances of firearms existing that were not listed on an official inventory. This was true for one of the three weapons attributed to the former SAC. We were also told that after FWS-OLE headquarters queried each region for a current inventory of their firearms for our assessment, one agent discovered his firearm had never been entered into either PPMS or LEMIS.

We found weaknesses in accounting for seized firearms converted to FWS property for undercover use during covert investigations. We found that FWS-OLE has no policy addressing the conversion of seized or forfeited firearms to government property. While many of these undercover firearms are received through forfeiture or court order, and are properly documented, others have no originating documentation. Undocumented firearms cannot be assigned a property number or tracked in PPMS. Without policy, undocumented firearms are not included in inventory lists and are not assigned property numbers.

Problems with accountability for firearms are not new to FWS. In 2003, a General Accounting Office (GAO) report stated that 18 federal agencies, including FWS, "could strengthen their controls in key areas important for effective inventory management." GAO specifically noted that FWS lacked written policies and procedures in several areas, including integrity of inventory and access to secured firearms. GAO also found that FWS could not account for 26 firearms. In response to this review, FWS officials identified how they would strengthen the firearms inventory program, including conducting unscheduled random checks of firearms and annual reviews of completed Reports of Survey for lost and stolen firearms. We found no evidence that these activities are occurring.

These weaknesses in accounting for firearms further emphasize the need for a formal quality control inspection program. Periodic independent inspections are critical to ensure that the proper inventory controls are in place and effective.

Recommendations

10. FWS-OLE should establish and maintain a complete and reliable inventory of firearms.

11. FWS-OLE should investigate all firearms inventory discrepancies in a timely manner, following their own established policies for investigating and reporting missing firearm incidents.

Converting Evidence to Property

We found a lack of control over government property that was formerly held as evidence or seized at ports of entry. Each year, FWS-OLE acquires thousands of wildlife products that are either illegal to possess or for other reasons cannot be returned to the owner. Most are forwarded to the Wildlife Repository, donated, or destroyed when no longer needed for investigative purposes. Others are maintained at local FWS-OLE offices for educational or display purposes.

FWS-OLE has no policy addressing the conversion of evidence or forfeited property to government ownership. Because the terms "educational" and "display" are not defined by policy, they are open to interpretation, resulting in varied applications. During our site visits, we found some FWS-OLE offices had few if any wildlife displays, while others were heavily adorned with an assortment of animal trophies, carved ivory tusks, bird mounts, and other wildlife products. Many of these items still have evidence tags attached, even though they are no longer being held as such, giving the appearance that evidence is being inappropriately handled.

Agents provided a variety of explanations for how these items are converted to government ownership and how they could be used once converted. We were told that the only set requirement is that the final disposition of the property must to be entered into the LEMIS system before the case can be closed. Often these items are placed on indefinite loan to other agencies; however, we found that there is no means to track this property once it is no longer in FWS-OLE's possession. One SAC we interviewed could not explain the process of converting evidence or otherwise non-returnable property to FWS-OLE ownership. When asked who makes the determination on what is kept for educational or display purposes, he stated, "That is a good question." He also acknowledged that FWS-OLE should come up with a better way of tracking educational and display items. We discovered that another SAC took action after our site visit by instructing offices within his region to no longer retain evidence once investigations are closed.

Recommendation

12. FWS-OLE should issue policy addressing the process of converting seized or forfeited property/evidence to FWS-OLE property. Policy should clearly define what is considered for display and educational purposes and create a uniform method to track and account for the property.

RESULTS OF EMPLOYEE SURVEY

We contracted with the Center for Ethical Business Cultures (CEBC), a nonprofit organization that provides assessment, ethical leadership development and consulting services, to develop and administer an employee survey. The survey was designed to provide us with an in-depth appraisal of FWS-OLE's ethical culture (See Appendices 2 and 3 for detailed survey results). We asked 369 FWS-OLE special agents and support staff to participate in the survey, and 325 responded; this response rate of 88 percent was much higher than we anticipated. The sizable response rate is beneficial for FWS-OLE management.

In analyzing the ethical culture of FWS-OLE, CEBC measured five core elements of the organization's culture:
- Stakeholder Commitment
- Mission, Vision and Values
- Trust, Integrity and Honesty
- Leadership
- Process Integrity

CEBC found the results of FWS-OLE's overall profile to be mixed. The first three themes emerged as strengths, the leadership theme had midrange results, and the process integrity theme clearly proved to be an area needing improvement. As defined by CEBC, process integrity means that an organization's "values, mission and vision are embedded within its culture and all of its organizational processes."

The survey results showed that employees are confident that their customers are satisfied with the products and services they receive. Employees also believe that they are good environmental stewards. Employees say that their own behaviors as well as their immediate managers' are consistent with the FWS-OLE mission. Most also report that coworkers have high ethical standards and that coworkers and immediate managers are trustworthy.

FWS-OLE employees are less positive with regard to senior management (FWS-OLE Chief and immediate staff). Specifically, senior leadership gets lower marks for trust and behaving in a way that is consistent with the mission. In addition, a large proportion of employees say that demonstrating values is not an important consideration in employee performance ratings or promotions and that communication is not shared freely. CEBC believes that given the importance of trust, leadership effectiveness, and process integrity as key ingredients in creating and sustaining ethical cultures, the problematic scores in these areas merit sustained attention by FWS-OLE.

19

RECOMMENDATIONS

Number	Recommendation	Page Number
1	FWS-OLE management should develop and execute plans to improve communication throughout the organization. Plans should consider periodic site visits by all levels of management, methods to identify and address employee concerns, and centralized methods for dissemination of agency information and policy.	7
2	FWS-OLE should issue policy addressing quality control inspection standards and requirements.	8
3	FWS-OLE should conduct formal quality control inspections annually and devise a plan for inspections to be completed at all FWS-OLE locations in the next 3 years.	8
4	FWS-OLE should create a formal leadership and management development program that values for both headquarters and field management experience.	10
5	FWS-OLE should monitor the issuance of performance awards to ensure consistency among regions and ensure that new Departmental standards are followed.	10
6	FWS-OLE should ensure all serious allegations are investigated by either the OIG or the PRU, or an appropriately trained and independent agent.	12
7	FWS-OLE should ensure that the PRU is provided with an annual budget to effectively plan and provide for necessary investigative work.	12
8	FWS-OLE should ensure that measures taken to hold employees accountable for their actions are carried out in a timely, fair, and consistent manner.	14
9	FWS-OLE should create a centralized system for handling and tracking disciplinary action of their sworn law enforcement personnel.	14
10	FWS-OLE should establish and maintain a complete and reliable inventory of firearms.	17
11	FWS-OLE should investigate all firearms inventory discrepancies in a timely manner, following their own established policies for investigating and reporting missing firearm incidents.	17
12	FWS-OLE should issue policy addressing the process of converting seized or forfeited property/evidence to FWS-OLE property. Policy should clearly define what are considered display and educational purposes and create a uniform method to track and account for the property.	18

FWS OFFICE OF LAW ENFORCEMENT FUNCTIONS

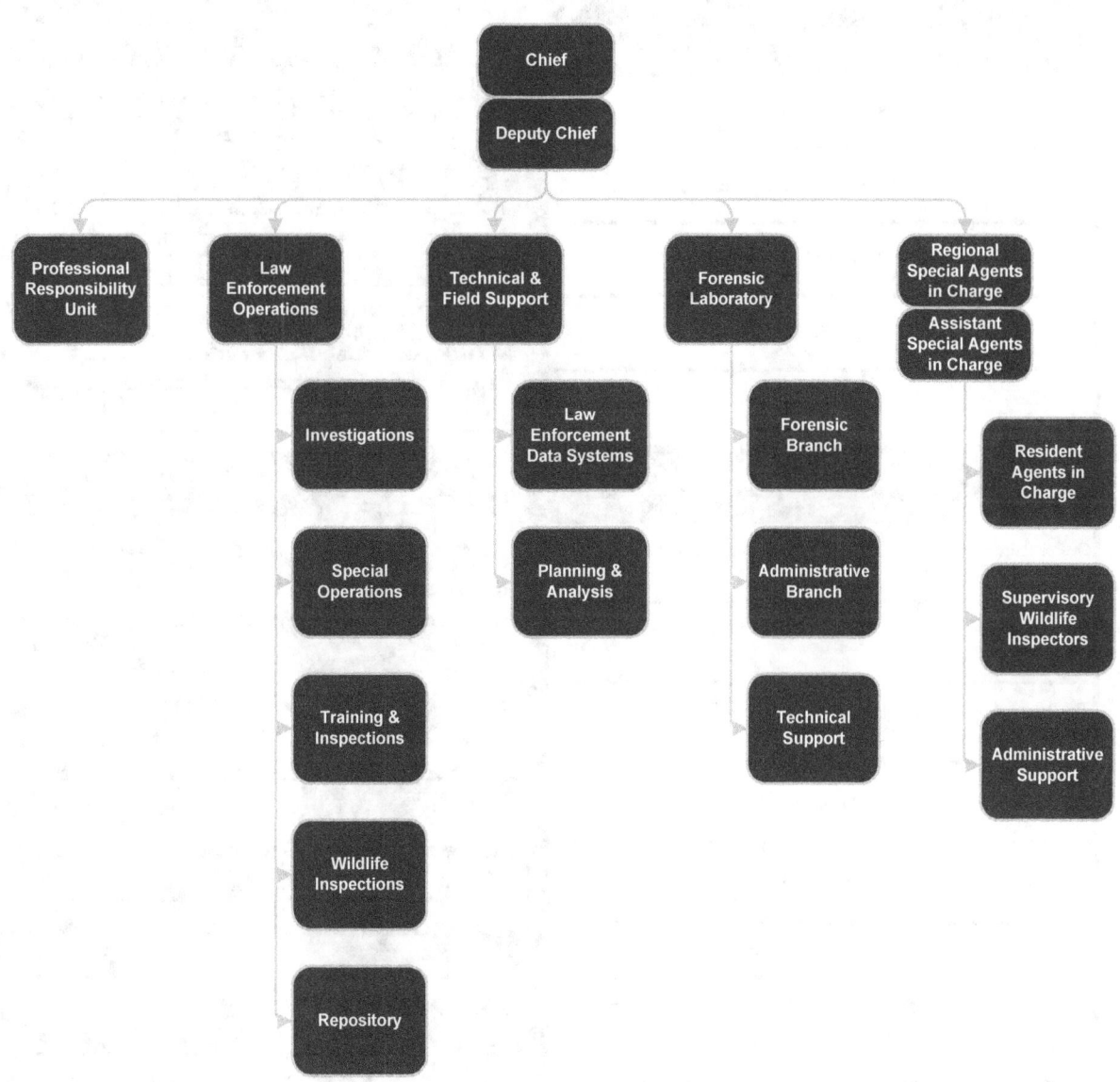

This is an abbreviated version of FWS-OLE's January 2006 Organizational Chart.

FWS-OLE EMPLOYEE SURVEY RESULTS

NATIONAL RESULTS

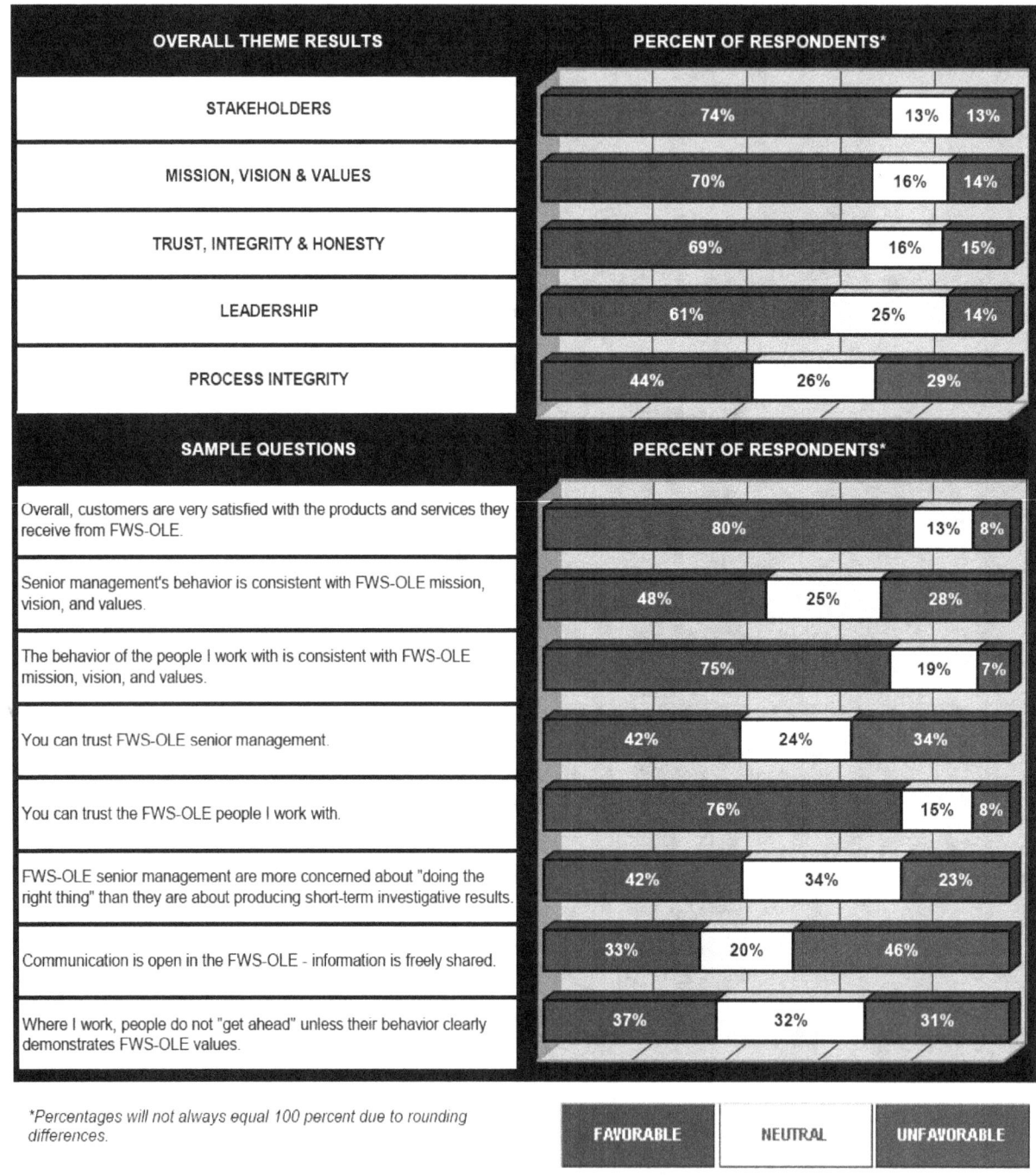

OVERALL THEME RESULTS	PERCENT OF RESPONDENTS*
STAKEHOLDERS	74% / 13% / 13%
MISSION, VISION & VALUES	70% / 16% / 14%
TRUST, INTEGRITY & HONESTY	69% / 16% / 15%
LEADERSHIP	61% / 25% / 14%
PROCESS INTEGRITY	44% / 26% / 29%

SAMPLE QUESTIONS	PERCENT OF RESPONDENTS*
Overall, customers are very satisfied with the products and services they receive from FWS-OLE.	80% / 13% / 8%
Senior management's behavior is consistent with FWS-OLE mission, vision, and values.	48% / 25% / 28%
The behavior of the people I work with is consistent with FWS-OLE mission, vision, and values.	75% / 19% / 7%
You can trust FWS-OLE senior management.	42% / 24% / 34%
You can trust the FWS-OLE people I work with.	76% / 15% / 8%
FWS-OLE senior management are more concerned about "doing the right thing" than they are about producing short-term investigative results.	42% / 34% / 23%
Communication is open in the FWS-OLE - information is freely shared.	33% / 20% / 46%
Where I work, people do not "get ahead" unless their behavior clearly demonstrates FWS-OLE values.	37% / 32% / 31%

*Percentages will not always equal 100 percent due to rounding differences.

FAVORABLE | NEUTRAL | UNFAVORABLE

FWS-OLE EMPLOYEE SURVEY RESULTS

REGIONAL RESULTS

SURVEY THEMES	NATIONAL	REGIONS							
		1	2	3	4	5	6	7	9/HQ
STAKEHOLDERS									
MISSION, VISION & VALUES									
TRUST, INTEGRITY & HONESTY									
LEADERSHIP									
PROCESS INTEGRITY									

SAMPLE QUESTIONS	NATIONAL	REGIONS							
		1	2	3	4	5	6	7	9/HQ
Overall, customers are very satisfied with the products and services they receive from FWS-OLE.									
Senior management's behavior is consistent with FWS-OLE mission, vision, and values.									
The behavior of the people I work with is consistent with FWS-OLE mission, vision, and values.									
You can trust FWS-OLE senior management.									
You can trust the FWS-OLE people I work with.									
FWS-OLE senior management are more concerned about "doing the right thing" than they are about producing short-term investigative results.									
Communication is open in the FWS-OLE - information is freely shared.									
Where I work, people do not "get ahead" unless their behavior clearly demonstrates FWS-OLE values.									

*Percentages will not always equal 100 percent due to rounding differences.

STRENGTH	NEUTRAL	OPPORTUNITY FOR IMPROVEMENT

www.ingramcontent.com/pod-product-compliance
Lightning Source LLC
Chambersburg PA
CBHW080941290526
45795CB00007BA/2843